ISBN 978-1-330-58625-9
PIBN 10036461

English
Français
Deutsche
Italiano
Español
Português

www.forgottenbooks.com

Mythology Photography **Fiction**
Fishing Christianity **Art** Cooking
Essays Buddhism Freemasonry
Medicine **Biology** Music **Ancient**
Egypt Evolution Carpentry Physics
Dance Geology **Mathematics** Fitness
Shakespeare **Folklore** Yoga Marketing
Confidence Immortality Biographies
Poetry **Psychology** Witchcraft
Electronics Chemistry History **Law**
Accounting **Philosophy** Anthropology
Alchemy Drama Quantum Mechanics
Atheism Sexual Health **Ancient History**
Entrepreneurship Languages Sport
Paleontology Needlework Islam
Metaphysics Investment Archaeology
Parenting Statistics Criminology
Motivational

LAYS

OF

KILLARNEY LAKES,

𝔇escriptive 𝔖onnets,

AND

OCCASIONAL POEMS.

BY

THOMAS GALLWEY, A.M.

With other ministrations thou, O Nature!
Healest thy wandering and distempered child:
Thou pourest on him thy soft influences,
Thy sunny hues, fair forms, and breathing sweets;
Thy melodies of woods and winds and waters!

COLERIDGE's "Remorse."

DUBLIN :

HODGES, FOSTER & CO., GRAFTON STREET,

PUBLISHERS TO THE UNIVERSITY.

1871.

CONTENTS.

———

OCCASIONAL PIECES.

Dedication.

To thee! light of my home, my heart, my life,

I bring the offspring of some careless hours,

Not cradled in sweet fancy's fairy bowers,

But in the sad resorts of care and strife.

These gifts to thee I bring, my own dear wife!

For they shall be to thee—like fresh-culled flowers

Still redolent of May and vernal showers—

With mutual thoughts and happy memories rife.

The many-pointed, many-wooded range

Of mountains, circling in all forms of grace

Round scenes, where lake and isle reflect each change

That courses through the sky with driving chase—

These in my mind have made a dwelling place;

What are they all without thy loved familiar face?

An Evening Ramble by the Lakes of Killarney.

I.

As once with closing day we strayed,
   My love and I, beside Loch-lein,*
Her gentle hand in mine she laid,
   And brought back vanished scenes again,
In words that breathed so soft a tone,
   They seemed but passing fancies wrought
By the mute promptings of my own
   Unconscious melancholy thought.

---

* The antient and appropriate name of Killarney Lakes.
So called in the Annals of Innisfallen, the Annals of the
Four Masters, and every other compilation not modern.
The name is derived from a small stream running down
Torc mountain. It is pronounced Lough-lane. (Note 21.)

B

Still evening o'er the landscape hung,
  Fringed by the light of parting day;
The rising moon of harvest flung
  The Castle's shadow o'er the bay;
The loveliest isle of all the isles
  That gem-like deck Loch-lein's fair breast,
Reflected still the lingering smiles,
  The farewell glances from the West.

" Tell me the tale of yon dear isle,
  Where we were wont to charm the hours
In musing o'er each ruined pile,
  And roaming through its hawthorn bowers."
So spoke her low sweet voice,—and I,
  Who would the happy dream prolong
Of those first days of wedded joy,
  Thus answer made in careless song.

𝕴nnisfallen. (1).

In the old, old days of Erin, when her life was
    in its prime,
(For the youngest days of nations are the eldest
    born of time)*
When the forest, and the covert for the wild-
    deer, reached the line,
Where the mountains' lofty summits into
    liquid light refine,
Innisfallen rested queen-like on her marble-
    founded throne,
Crowned with light from emerald bowers,
    cinctured by her crystal zone.
There, whilst over half the nations feebly glim-
    mered twilight wan,

* Antiquitas sæculi juventus mundi.

Shone, matured to noontide brilliance, light—
    the quickening life of man.
There too workers, meek and holy, bending
    o'er the deathless page,
Garnered up, for future story, fruit from each
    successive age.*

Vain, alas! the hope, the promise,—soon, too
    soon, the vernal bloom,
Rudely dashed by soiling fingers, sought the
    dark and silent tomb.
Brief, loved isle, thy tide of glory l ebbing once,
    it ceased to flow;
Crumbling pile, and mouldering ruin, mark
    thy thousand years of woe.
Still men say that phantom-spirits haunt thy
    crystal-cinctured shore,

* The Annals of Innisfallen.

Midnight strains of music mingling with the
distant torrent's roar.

I remember! I remember! what in after days
befel,
When the hunter searched the mountains, and
the bugle note the dell,
Gaily flew the streaming pennons, fleets of
barges thronged the bay,
And ten thousand eager faces marked the
coming of the prey.
Here he comes! the antlered monarch, with an
eye and front sublime,
Like a herald bearing tidings from men of the
old, old time.
Hark the cry! he shall not perish! through
his wild woods let him roam!
And Loch-lein! thy bounding waters bear
the monarch to his home.

Now away ! away ! returning, shoots each
  homeward-veering skiff,

As the bugle sounds the signal from the chapel
  on the cliff,

And the queenly island echoes mirth and music
  o'er the wave,

From the gentle and the simple, from the
  lovely and the brave.

But 'tis gone, the fairy vision which my
  wayward fancy saw ;

With changed times we too are changing, 'tis
  a universal law ;

Save alone the peerless island, with its beauty
  ever new,

Yet old as the circling waters, or the heaven's
  o'erarching blue.

II.

" Oh ! turn not yet from yonder shore,
   While peals far off the vesper chime,
But sing me from the island lore,
   Some legend of the old, old time."
So spoke the same soft voice again,
   And I, the thrall of her sweet will,
Searched through the fancies of my brain,
   And found a chord responsive still.

The Legend of Father Cuddy. (2).

———

O'ER the starry vault of Heaven streams the
    moonbeam's silver flood,
Tracing forth in softest outline, mountain,
    island, lake, and wood,
And the castle grandly looming, with its
    barbicon and fosse—
(Ah ! more potent now in ruin, ivy-mantled
    tower of Rosse).

O'er the waters sweetly floating, comes the
    midnight call to prayer,
Raising human hearts to Heaven, drawing
    spirits down from air ;
Interchange of earth with Heaven, passing as
    the passing bell,

But around yon isle of beauty, casting then a
    living spell.

For, responsive to the summons, see a light
    skiff passes o'er,
From its moorings by the mainland, Innisfallen !
    to thy shore.
Wan and wasted is its tenant, though in sooth
    he little deems
That he comes back from long tarrying in the
    shadow-land of dreams.

Him no eye of kindness welcomes, but mute
    records of the dead,
And the stare from wondering faces meet his
    troubled gaze instead.
Lo ! the sappling by him tended stands aloft a
    giant oak ;
And the tree wherein he sheltered long has
    felt the woodman's stroke.

Altered words and foreign accents bring no
    greeting to his ears,
All is changed save he the changeless, in the
    long, long lapse of years.
Like a mass of rock primeval breaking through
    a newer zone,
He among, but still not of them, stands un-
    friended and alone.

Soon he feels his spirit ebbing from its
    tenement of clay,
Dust to dust collapsing quickly; but the soul
    pursues its way,
Moving onward to the mansions never changing,
    ever new,
Home of old divinely promised to the meek,
    the pure, the true.

Still the dweller by these waters, simple-
    minded, fancy-free,

At the witching hour of midnight, as he
lingers on the lea,
Sees the light skiff with its tenant wan and
wasted passing o'er,
From its moorings by the mainland, isle of
beauty! to thy shore.

III.

" See now the moon is at its height,
    And lights the Castle walls across ;
Tell me of his, the Chieftain's, flight
    From yonder ivied Keep of Ross,
Who gave to all the region round
    His name, a living memory."
She spoke, and at the whispered sound,
    I told this tale as told to me.

Legend of O'Donoghue of Ross. (3).

LIKE an eagle o'er its eyrie, newly poised upon
    the wing,
On the verge of towering ramparts stood erect
    the wizard king,
All around him stretched the forest, over
    mountain, over plain;
At his feet his fairy palace, in the depths of
    fair Loch-Lein.

Once he dwelt beneath those waters, but for-
    sook his spirit-race,
Lured by light from heaven beaming on an
    earth-born maiden's face.
She was lovely, but as fleeting as the cloudless
    dawn of day,

When the spring, with wild-flowers laden,

    comes to greet the laughing May.

For his love was more than mortals', and she

    faded soon in air,

As the tender dew drop passes in the noontide's

    sultry glare.

Passing fair are Loch-lein's waters, passing

    fair its starry isles;

Softest zephyrs float around them, Flora there

    perpetual smiles;

Lofty mountains, nobly out-lined, guard fond

    nature's treasured love,

And sweet Echo, softly soothing, music makes

    thro' hill and grove.

But for *him*, the lonely elf-king, beauty blooms

    on earth no more,

When the light of love had left him, naught

    could beauty's sense restore.

Now his courser from the ramparts, thither
    brought by mystic spells,
Bears him downward thro' the waters to the
    halls where Echo dwells.
There sweet Echo soothes his sorrow, calls in
    tones once-loved his name,
And the shape he cherished taking, gives him
    back an answering flame.

Still as each recurring season ushers in the
    halcyon May,
Milk-white coursers bear the elf-king, bear
    him thro' the silvery spray,
To the scenes where earth's fair daughter
    shared his more than mortal love,
While the elf-band scatter favours where his
    light-winged coursers move.

IV.

"Now silence spreads from shore to shore
  A sense of awe which is not fear,
And even the torrent's distant roar,
  More silent makes the silence here."
Then I—"that torrent's roar I deem
  The forward notes that hither come
To herald in the parent stream,
  That seeks in fair Loch-lein a home.
Then dream we on our evening dream,
  And by its bank in fancy roam."

The River Flesk. (4).

———

BUBBLING up among the mountains, at the
gate-ways of the day,*

First it trickles from its fountains, as a child
first feels its way;

Quickly gains it speed and volume, and rolls
merrily along,

Perfect image of the boyhood of a joyous child
of song;

For it kisses, as it passes, flowery bank and
drooping spray

And each streamlet from the mountains sent
to speed it on its way.

* "Gate-ways of the day,"—the reader will doubtless
recognise this phrase from Tennyson's Locksley Hall.

Now, like Samson blind and captive, from his
    bed among the rocks
See the river-god, uprising, shakes his liberated
    locks,
And assails the deep foundation of the rock-
    built robber's den;
Rushes onwards, bearing havoc, to the dwellers
    in the glen.

Slowly gliding, gently winding, now it seeks
    some calm retreat
Where the wild ash hangs its berries, and the
    oak and holly meet;
There prepares the pebbly pavement, in its
    pools below the wood
For the pride of all the waters—silver monarch
    of the flood.

If the golden orb be setting, with full splen-
    dour, in the west,

And the busy voice of nature, save its waters',
    is at rest;
Then this river blows a trumpet, making
    music of its own,
Now approaching, now receding in a pleasant
    monotone;
And the blazing splendour flashes from *the*
    Castle (5) on the height ;
'Tis the glory of the river, and the home of
    calm delight.

Name not here in words outspoken, who are
    Lord and Lady there,
But the thought will bring unbidden to my
    lips the earnest prayer,
That its towers may ever flourish, its broad
    woods be ever green,
And the gentle life within it ever harmonize
    the scene.

Now once more unto the river! see it hastens
    on amain

To the goal of all its longings, the sweet bosom
    of Loch-lein ;

There it courses through the Eden where the
    pleasant waters throng,

Guarded round by comely mountains, lulled
    by echo's sweetest song,

And recounts the varied marvels that befel it
    on its way

From its bubbling crystal fountain at the
    gate-ways of the way.

v.

" No single fount with tribute feeds
    The brimming bosom of Loch-lein;
The waving corn has many seeds,
    And many a fount the watery plain."

Straight rose the vision to my mind
Of that sweet spot where Scotland's pride, (6)
The household friend of all mankind,
Enraptured viewed the double tide.

The Old Weir Bridge. (7).

In beauty's bowers there be many fairest spots
　　among the fair,
Food for after-thoughts and day-dreams, hints
　　for castles built in air,
Pleasant places in the vista leading back to
　　bygone years,
Lights amid thick-coming shadows, smiles
　　across fast-falling tears.

Such a spot of peerless beauty comes across
　　my fancy now,
Like a gem of faultless lustre sparkling on a
　　queenly brow ;
Low-browed arches, pent-up waters, foaming
　　o'er the barrier-ridge,
Named a name which tells its story, named of
　　old the Old Weir Bridge.

Here they come, the gallant bargemen! each
    reclining on his oar,
With the mountain-wall for back-ground,
    and the tranquil pools before ;
Gaily bounding shoots the vessel to the haven
    of its rest,
Darting swiftly through the rapids, like a
    falcon to its nest.

Mark the green leaves of the forest kiss the
    river as it flows!
Mark the pine-wood on the island where it
    seeks a brief repose!
Brief repose and hasty parting! here the stream
    divides in twain,
Flowing eastward, flowing westward, ne'er to
    meet but in the main.

So are parted kindred spirits on the current
    stream of life,

Some divided by ill-fortune, others by a petty
strife;

Others to the land of shadows, fate relentless
calls away,

Whilst the loved ones and the lovely vainly
bid the doomed one stay.

Old Weir Bridge! once through these waters
England's Queen came gaily down,*

By her sat one loved and trusted, bearing sway
without a crown;

Few short moons had waned in heaven, ere
the splendid dream had fled,

England's Queen was steeped in sorrow, lowly
lay the uncrowned head.

* Allusion is here made to the " shooting of the bridge,"
as the passing under it is called, by her Majesty the Queen,
on the 27th August, 1861, during the visit with which she
honoured Lord and Lady Castlerosse.

VI.

" Methinks my fancy can descry
    Two types of beauty native here,
The soaring eagle for the eye,
    And sweet-toned echo for the ear.
For king and queen they well might stand,
    To poets' eye in olden time,
Of this enchanted fairy-land!"
    I caught and turned the thought to rhyme.

The Eagle's Nest. (8).

ONCE sweet Echo and the Eagle had their dwell-
    ings side by side
In a rock beside a river with a gently winding
    tide;
In a rock which rose to Heaven like a trophy
    from the ground
With green banners gaily streaming and with
    oak and ivy crowned.

When the infant world was forming here
    young Echo dwelt alone,
Watching early nature's lispings, making every
    voice her own.
Once she heard an Eagle screaming as he
    soared to view the sky,
And gave back the sound with rapture, answer-
    ing with her mimic cry.

As he heard the mimic accents through the
    azure blithely run,
Straight he staid his golden pinions on their
    journey toward the sun;
Downward swooping, soon he rested on the
    rock whence came the calls,
And unconscious fixed his eyrie 'mid sweet
    Echo's tuneful halls.

Many chambers had sweet Echo, reaching up
    from foot to crest,
But one only had the Eagle for his imme-
    morial nest;
And sweet Echo wooed the Eagle through the
    portals of his ears
With the pealings of the thunder, grand old
    music from the spheres.

There for ages dwelt together nature's well-
    assorted pair,

'Till low aims and human folly scared the bird
    who rules the air.
Since then Echo sits there lonely, by the gently
    winding stream,
Only in the distance hearing, not for her, the
    Eagle scream.

So high hopes too often vanish, passing shapes
    of Heaven-sent truth,
Balmy breath of early morning, soft and
    downy bloom of youth;
And sharp pangs of wasting sorrow cast their
    shadows in between,
While sad memory tells, like Echo, not what is
    but what hath been.

VII.

  " The night with all its starlight glory
    Now robes the calmly sleeping lake,
  And on each cliff and promontory
    Ever and anon the ripples break

Most drowsily, as though to mark
    The hour for him to seek repose
Who would awaken with the lark,
    And crown day's labour by its close.

" See where the broad-backed Mangerton
    Looms in the sky-line to the east;
Recall the wrong by Saxon done
    To peasant's faith and Celtic priest
Within yon mountain's peaceful dell,—
    A wrong may ne'er be done again!"
My lips obeyed the soft-voiced spell,
    And thus I sung my farewell strain.

The Mangerton Hymn. (9).

WE will go unto God's altar at the breaking of
the day,

Whilst the dew is on the heather and the mist
hangs round our way;

We will go unto God's altar, where the sun-
beams longest shine

And woods and winds and waters sing a
melody divine.

How we loved thy temple's beauty, where our
fathers oft have knelt,

Regal shrines by mighty masters, where,
O Lord! thy glory dwelt!

But the glory is departed, and the beauty
passed away

To the field among the mountains where we
meet and kneel to-day.

Gently judge thy faithful people; mark us out
    among our foes:
Faith is now our only portion, they on all we
    lost repose;
Crimson-handed, iron-hearted, they raise high
    the clang of might
O'er the voice of pleading reason and the gen-
    tle rule of right.

We are landless, we are homeless, our sole
    dwelling in the cave,
And the shadow of yon Abbey, by the Yew-
    tree, in the grave.
Show us there is balm in Gilead, pour on age
    the light of truth,
And the flood of clear keen joyance on the
    stainless heart of youth.

We will sing—tho' now in sorrow—joyous
    songs of hope and praise

'Til each rock in hill and hollow gives us back
  the shout we raise;
For thy saving face shines on us, casting
  stedfast light before,
As we journey thro' the desert to the land we
  loved of yore.

" Now doth the gorse from many a hill
  The night with heavy fragrance woo,
And every herb doth now distil
  The clear, cold, bead of silver dew.
'Twere·time at last we farewell bade
  To lingering steps and careless song."—
" But not for long," her sweet voice said,
  And echo answered, not for long!

Sonnets.

The Mountains called " The Paps"—in Irish " Da Cic," literally the two Breasts. (10).

In bold relief against the eastern sky,

The twin, vast, rounded summits towering stand,

Like giant warders of the Fairy land

Which lies beneath; or, to the Celtic eye,

Like holiest types of blest maternity.

Here once, whence beauty's lines serenely grand

In circles over heaven and earth expand,

The Queen of spells her palace reared on high.

Would'st trace the past in monumental stone

And shadowy outlines of primeval man,

These heights ascend, when noon-tide heat has flowr

And ruins bleached by countless winters scan;

Then sit and muse on Rites and Races gone,

As I do now, sad, silent and alone.

D

Gleann-na-Coppull. (11).

(THE HORSE'S GLEN).

———

UNKNOWN, untrodden by the foot of man,
Glen of the triple lakes, and barriers high—
Wave-washed below and cloud-capped in the sky—
Thy wild flowers bloom where late the torrent ran,
Thy garden shapes itself by nature's plan.
Like buried gold thy charms unheeded lie,
Save when the mountaineer with wondering eye
Pauses to view the rainbow's glittering span.
Child of the hills! new risen with the day,
I see him o'er the heathery mountains flit,
I see him mark the many-colored ray,
Light in his eye and native mother wit;
Behold! the Bow which lured him turns to grey,
And he too passes with its hues away.

Benaunmore. (12).

—

Now Benaunmore is bathed in summer haze;
Below fast-cradled in its rocky dell
Loch Carrig-vea sleeps motionless and well;
High over-head the massive columns raise,
Tier above tier, memorials of old days,
When nature's early throes and labors fell
Framed the cool grot and close-sequestered cell
Whereon the world's wanderer loves to gaze.
Oh! never surely, in her fondest mood,
Did nature build for man her sovran child,
A more alluring home where solitude
Might win him to his better self; beguiled,
By concord sweet of mountain, lake, and wood,
To blend the grandly fair and greatly good.

The Killarney Echo.

ROUSED from her couch beside the silent shore,

Where full-caparisoned her coursers stay,

She bears her message o'er the waveless bay,

Tells it in mountain-hall and cavern hoar,

By murmuring brook, still lake, and torrent's roar;

Peak after peak she passes in array,

Then rushes o'er the hills and far away,

'Till circling home she sinks to earth once more.

Echo! the place made vocal by thy strain

Is hallowed ground whereon our spirits feel

The thrill of long forgotten joy or pain—

The bugle-note, the cannon's deafening peal,

The full-voiced chorus, and the wild refrain,

And ah! *one* voice that ne'er shall speak again.

Caran-tual. (13).

———

I saw the summer sun go down behind the sea,
And o'er the pale moon grow a golden light,
From lonely Caran-tual's topmost height
Towering aloft in cloudless majesty ;
The serried hills beneath seem in the night
Like billowy ocean, heaving in its might
And turned to stone ; while far as eye can see
The lengthening shadows o'er the surface flee.
Around, each crag and jutting fragments tell
The name and features of the beldam old,
Potent in herbs and versed in many a spell
Who dwelt unblest within her mountain hold.
Oh blame not if each shadow as it fell
Seemed the weird phantom of the haunted dell !

Caher Con-righ. (14).

———

His heart was fashioned in heroic mould
Who fixed his eyrie on this cloud-capped rock,
Scorning the wild waves' roar and tempest's shock;
The better thus in one wide glance to hold
The ocean track, from where full Shannon rolled,
To that lone isle where first the billows broke
Their gathered strength, whilst sheltering coves inv
The dauntless rovers on the watery wold.
Full many a time and oft, across the main,
From this high tower, the watchman's sleepless que
Descried the swarming fleets of sunny Spain,
Urged on by fate to seek the utmost West.
E'en now as further lands are yet to gain,
No stop, no stay, 'tis Westward Ho! again.

Dunlo Castle. (15).

High on a cliff, thy gray square tower, Dunlo!
O'erhangs the darkly-rolling, eddying Laune,
And fronts the mountain-gorge with threatening fro
As tho' in menace of the native foe;
For hence "the Stranger" dealt out many a blow,
And from this stand-point drove the iron brand
Home to the heart of a distracted land.
Such musings from thy outward aspect grow,—
But turn within, and words will not define
The house-hold charm which breathes from all arou
Here past and present mutely blending join
To build sweet home on immemorial ground,
—Joy of young hearts and dear to life's decline—
Long may'st thou guard the fondly cherished line!

Aghadoe. (16).

———

WITHIN the compass of this narrow spot,

Remorseless ruin holds her wasting reign

O'er dungeon-Keep, round-Tower and holy Fane;

The men who made and marred them both forgot,

Their lineage, name, date, place, remembered not.

Still fancy deems the Lord of fair Loghlein

Might bless and rule from here his wide domain,

At once a Priest and Chieftain of the Scot.

No more the yews' twin shadows may return

To mark the field from nature named of old,

But through all time the pilgrims steps shall learn

To haunt the sunny slopes which hold

The loved and lost whom now the people mourn,

Deeming these walls one vast sepulchral urn.

The Abbey of Irrelagh. (17).

(MUCKROSS ABBEY).

———

YES! they were men of a diviner mind,

Who sought and found ideal beauty here,

A breathing harmony from Heaven's own sphere;

Where the poor, cowled, and cloistered monk combi

The love of heaven with love of his own kind.

Such didst thou once, loved Irrelagh! appear,

Such wert thou still through many a changing year

'Till the rude spoiler scattered to the wind

Thy gentle sway.   But not for aye the prize

Remains, unchallenged, to mere force alone;

Perennial spring all human sympathies,

And good men's deeds for foul misdeeds atone—

Behold again loved Irrelagh arise,

And lifts its beacon-light, to lure us to the skies!

Derrynane Abbey.

THE RESIDENCE OF O'CONNELL.

Ye ocean gales, blow gently o'er these lone
And silent halls! ye ocean waves rejoice
Low murmuring! for here HE tuned his voice—
Now soft as notes of lover's lute to one
Who tarries long to hear; and now a tone
Fanning the breath of battle—*Here* slow grew
His mind to its full compass, till he drew
Within its ample folds, the wealth unknown
Of Celtic story; here He learned the lore
Of antique liberty; hence issuing forth
He broad-cast flung from his abounding store
Through all his native land, from south to north,
Fair freedom's seed, and coloured to the core
Her wild, sweet heart, thus never wooed before.

Roman Catholic Cathedral.

KILLARNEY.

THE beauty of the everlasting hills—
Now here with many a peak sublimely crowned,
Now there in undulations winding round,
And feeding, as they wind, with thousand rills,
The cradled lake below—with rapture fills
The gazer's heart; but may not wholly sound
Of human consciousness the deep profound,
That at the beatific vision thrills.
So haply deem the great, wise men who rear,
Within the shadow of the mountain's brow,
A temple meet for such a spot, severe,
And inornate, where every knee may bow
In adoration of the far brought near,
Or music lift the soul to her harmonious sphere.

St. Ann's Lying-in Hospital, Killarney.

(Established in 1865 by the Viscountess Castlerosse.)

STRANGER stay, nor pass with heedless eye
Yon modest mansion; mark its cold, grey wall!
'Tis worthier far than lordliest hall
Whate'er thou hast of human sympathy;
For therein new-born babe and mother lie
Delicately tended, screened from all
The thousand pangs and perils that befall
The houseless poor, when that dread hour draws nig
That hour obedient to the high decree,
Which brings in sorrow forth to life and light
Creation's marvel, the epitome
Of nature's self, where Heaven and Earth unite.
Lo! here reposes on the mother's knee
Her new-found bliss, the heir of all eternity.

St. Joseph's Industrial School, Killarney.

(Established in 1867 by the Viscountess Castlerosse.)

———

To *stamp* on childhood's eager plastic mind
A Father's image, truer (tho' supreme)
Than his, on whom the Orphan in its dream
Nightly, with unavailing love, reclined;
To *show* the young, that heart and hand combined
Reveal the hidden meaning of the theme,
Wherein the cloistered sages say they deem
That Prayer and labor are the same in kind;
T'*impart* the varied household arts that span,
With arch of rain-bow hues, the wide abyss
Parting the age of rude, primeval man,
From modes of life which mould and govern this—
Such roll to fill unbidden, is to be
A worker true, a hand-maid of the Deity.

Lunatic Asylum:

KILLARNEY.

———

Oh! ne'er did nature in her softest mood

A fairer banquet to the sight supply

Than spreads itself beneath this palace high,

Unreason's home—the Giver of all good

Who gives each sense its own peculiar food,

Here reaches, through the gate-way of the eye,

Reason, unthroned, or fixed in vacancy,

Or lost mid dream-lands insubstantial brood.

A tree, a flower, the thin blue wreath of smoke,

Seen afar off against the mountain's slope,

May banished scenes and memories lost evoke,

To chase the fiend with which 'twere vain to cope,

And win dear reason back.—A flash, a stroke,

When cannon failed, has deepest slumber broke!

Sister Agnes. (18).

————

HER eyes are lit with calm unconscious light,
Such radiance as illumes the burnished west
When sunset brings to toil the hour of rest;
From her close hood no tress escapes to view,
Tho' fancy deems it silken, whatso'er the hue;
Her smile sheds sunshine on the stricken breast,
Her voice seems melody itself comprest
To its prime essence—such the being bright,
By strength invisible who walks secure
Thro' courts and camps and lowly haunts
Of fevered misery, intent to pour
The oil and wine for whoso solace wants—
'Tis Sister Agnes! friend of rich and poor,
The bride of Heaven, *la sœur de bon secours.*

Contents.

———

Joy, unalloyed by pain, is rare to find.

The chance unveiling of long hidden love;

In danger's searching hour, the quick resolve;

A law of nature, big with change, divined;

A battle fought and won, to save mankind;

Sudden to meet, when crowds unfriendly prove,

The tender gaze we set all store above;

These call up joy, but care rides post behind.

Now pass we in review the convent-roll;

There joy unwavering meets us face to face,

For there the all-but disembodied soul

Communes with beings of a kindred race,

And every act tends onward to the goal

Beyond the bigot's ken or statesman's vain control.

Association of Ideas.

———.

I hear the Silent, in the tempest's roar,

In the low music of the evening's sigh,

In thunder pealing thro' the nether sky,

In the loud boom along the rock-bound shore,

In insects' hum, when thro' the bowers they pour

On drowsy lids their noontide lullaby;

I see th' Unseen, when dawn first meets the eye

On ocean's verge; I see it evermore

Within the clear obscure of starry night,

And in the lowly, flower-embroidered plain,

In roused Atlantic surging to its height,

And in thy placid depths—beloved Loughlein!—

What'er awakens awe or yields delight

Stirs a new life in hearing and in sight.

Life and Death.

———

SOME die, cut off in full and bounding life
And strength of thought; with such, the beacon-light
Of many a heart is quenched in sudden night,
Mayhap the quiet of a home and darling wife,
The clash of mind with mind, the glorious strife,
Which prompts ambition's most ennobling flight
To combat wrong and set the wronger right—
These seem to die, but leave the world still rife
With their o'ermastering presence.   Some again
Survive their proper selves, and manhood's bloom,
'Till of the paragon doth nought remain,
But palsy creeping to the joyless tomb.
Then strike no balance here of loss and gain,
'Tis only after death that all shall be made plain.

The Catastrophe.

(*Written after the Surrender at Sedan, September,* 1870).

———

A STAR that gemmed the forehead of the sky,

A grace that clothed in beauty whatsoe'er

It touched, a fragrance filling all the air,

Vanished from earth, and like a dream passed by,

What time the Gaul, remorseless Lord of war

And pleasure's slave, went forth on conquest's car,

(Embattled squadrons daring to defy)

And fell all-blasted from his flight on high.

Fair France! thy sensuous rule is o'er; for lo!

Thine idol's vaunted laurels are the foil

To feet of clay; thy cheek's voluptuous glow

Surmounts the sinuous serpent's scaly coil;

On waxen pinions thou would'st heavenward go;

Thy guerdon is—unutterable woe.

France.

(Written after the Surrender of Metz, 29th October, 1870.)

——

PEAL after peal reverb'rates through the sky,

Sounding the tocsin of a nation's doom—

Its name and fortunes buried in the gloom

Of anarchy, and never more to ply

The bloody trade of war, or reassume

The flush of life, new-risen from the tomb

Of dark oblivion, where, when empires die,

The shattered fragments of dominion lie.

Persia, the Mede, Chaldæa, Carthage, Rome,

Poland and Spain have vanished in the past;

Another now, dearer and nearer home,

Is blotted out, smit by the furnace blast

Of desolation.   Thence no more shall come

The cannon's roar, the trumpet-call, or beat of drum.

Victor Emmanuel enters Rome at the head of the Revolution.

———

METHINKS I see the founder of old Rome,

(By she-wolf suckled, stained by brother's blood,

King o'er the gathered outlaws' robber brood)

A phantom grim now hovering o'er the dome

Which faith has hallowed, genius made the home

Of worshippers, and in exultant mood,

As in the days of Jove viewing the flood

Of midnight murder, fraud, and rapine come

With him mis-called Emmanuel. But no!

The stream of time will not roll back its course;

Nor human breast the hope assured forego

That moral right will conquer lawless force;

All else shall pass, thrones fall, and kingdoms sever,

The promise is—for ever and for ever!

On Prince Arthur's Departure from Killarney,
APRIL, 1869.

———

THE time will come when other scenes than these
Will compass thee and fill thine eye and heart
When centred in the great world's greatest mart,
Where meet all joys of sense and arts that please,
Borne from all lands and over all the seas.
In splendour's midst, of which thou'lt be a part,
(And noblest one, if thou but faithful art
To youthful promise) suffer not to cease
From memory's teeming page, the circling zone
Of mountain peaks, the lake of many isles,
Sweet echo imaging the bugle's tone,
The pleasant ramble in the steep defiles,
The cheer that welcomed in the Royal Son,
The farewell greeting to thyself alone.

Occasional Pieces.

TO THE HON. MARGARET BROWNE, AGED EIGHT YEARS
DAUGHTER OF LORD AND LADY CASTLEROSSE.

The Daisy, the Pearl, and Marguerite.*

1.

A FLOWER it is that comes before
    The thrush is on the wing,
A link between the winter hoar,
    And happy hours of spring.
The skies of night are not more bright
    When spangled o'er with gold,
Than lawn and lea when decked with thee,
    First offspring of the wold!

---

* Marguerite, Fr. for daisy, Margarita, Lat., and Marga-
rites, Grk. for pearl.

2.

A GEM it is that hath its birth
   Beneath the ocean waves;
It grows to beauty, size and worth
   Within the coral caves.
The milky way in bright array
   Spanning the world beneath,
Is not more fair than raven hair,
   Bearing the pearly wreath!

3.

Fair daughter of an ancient line!
   They bade, in happiest hour,
The sweetly-burthened name be thine,
   Pearl of the House and Flower!
May earth and air their blessings bear
   To thee, bright flower of love!
May the deep sea send bliss to thee,
   And Heaven the teaching dove!

Laying the first stone of Derrycunnihy Chapel.

The incident here related occurred on the occasion when the Hon. Margaret Browne (8 years old) laid the foundation stone of Lady Castlerosse's Chapel, on the lofty eminence overlooking Derrycunnihy Cottage. The words attributed to the little founder were spoken, and the reason of the name given, by the little Lady without a moment's hesitation.

'Tis here beside this guarding rock,
　　Thus far upon the height
Which backwards rolls the tempest's shock,
　　We mark the chosen site.
Yon gentle child shall turn the sod,
　　And lay the parent stone,
For here we build a house to God,
　　The reflex of His throne.

Oh! deem it not a fancy wild
　　That spirits from the sphere,
In hovering o'er that gentle child,
　　Made music in her ear!
For hark! the little maid exclaimed,
　　" Thou shalt be called from high
" Saint Mary of the angels,—named
　　" As neighbour to the sky!'"

Oh! long may wave o'er glen and glade
　　The many-tinted woods!
Long wildly leap in broad cascade
　　The darkly-rolling floods!
And long be heard through all the vale
　　Her voice in Sabbath bells
Sing " Mary of the angels, hail! "
　　And run through all the dells.

The Killarney Boatmen's Song,

Commemorative of Her Excellency the Countess Spencer's Visit to the Lakes in April, 1869.

———

To our oars! to our oars!
There's a fairy on the lake;
To our oars! to our oars!
We must follow in her wake.

Can you tell, can you tell
Is she dark or is she fair?
Does she come, can you say,
From the earth or from the air?

She is fair, she is fair,
As the dawning of the day,
And she comes, oh! she comes
From the cradle of the May.

In her eye is a beam
From the setting of the sun,
And her smile caught its ray
When his race had just begun.

In her voice is a note
From the warble of the bird
Which makes musical the night
Where his melody is heard.

And of late when she passed
O'er the daisies on the lawn,
They believed that they felt
But the shadow of the dawn!

From Mulla* is a voice,
Ever singing in her train,

* Mulla is the antient name of the river now called Aubeg,
on whose banks Spenser composed his Faerie Queene.

'Tis the Queen, Fairy Queen,
Come to visit us again!

And a voice from the shore,
At the close of every strain,
Calls out, " Queen, Fairy Queen,
Come to visit us again."

So to oars! to our oars!
There's a fairy on the lake,
To our oars! to our oars!
We must follow in her wake.

Long Ago.

———

Long ago! When was that? it was when
We were boys, and we thought ourselves men;
When the hope of our life was sublime
And we ne'er thought the joy of our prime
          Would seem so
          Long ago!

There's a face, very grave, very mild,
Gazing down on the couch of a child,
With the eyes, very dark, full of play;
'Tis a face that still haunts me to-day
          Though she's low
          Long ago.

Many years, unperceived, have gone by,
Since my love, yes my love! you and I
Were by fate, happy fate! joined together;
Should our life flow along thus for ever,
      We'll not know
      Long ago.

In fair France the six months are an age
Since the King first took up the war-gage;
But the blood, and the shame, and the pain,
Ever-green, ever-fresh, shall remain,
      And ne'er grow
      Long ago.

'Tis the heart is the true test of time;
As it beats, so we run or we climb;
As our joy gives to years their light wings,
From one hour of great grief there up-springs,
      With its woe,
      Long ago.

A True Story.

———

THERE dwelt in a cottage beside a brook
  ·A grey-haired recluse bent double with years;
A gold-headed staff and emblazoned book
      Were the sole remains
      From wide domains
    Lavished in youth on his gay compeers.

By the old man's side, there silently grew
  A blooming child, then a maiden fair;
The light of her eyes was a violet hue,
      And every fold
      Reflected gold
    From each wavy tress of her auburn hair.

An oak hard-by, all gnarled and bare,

  An ever-green's tendrils lovingly bound,

('Twas the last of a forest that once grew there)—

    Thus the maiden wound

    His old heart round

  With her violet eyes and golden hair.

A Knight coming by in evil hour

  Harried the heart of this motherless fair,

And lured her away to his lonely tower;—

    The old heart broke

    Beneath the stroke

  Which severed the bond of the golden hair.

Thus, long ago, was a grand-sire slain

  By a belted knight from his fort in the hills,

—The hills which circle the fair Loch-lein—

    Ah! crueller far

    Than scath of war

  Is the base contriver of home-spun ills.

Marathon.

April 29*th*, 1870.

———

But yesterday thou wert a star
    Radiant to every clime,
A spell, to rouse the heart in war,
    To build the loftiest rhyme!

A household word, a golden link
    Drawn out from age to age,
For all who greatly do and think
    Upon the world's wide stage!

But now, that latest deed annuls
    The Persian's famous grave,   .
Thou Golgotha, thou place of skulls,
    Thou lair for Thug and slave!

Innisfallen.

Just thirteen hundred years gone-by,
  Ere Echo's tuneful halls
Save to the welkin made reply
  And wild deer's clamorous calls;

Like Eden in a solitude,
  Or gem of purest ray,
Or star the first in magnitude,
  The lovely island lay—

Lay guarded by its zone of mountains,
  Lay on thy crystal plain
—Fed by a thousand teeming fountains—
  Oh! grandly fair Loch-lein!

There thither led by voice divine,
　　Saint Finan ceased his quest,
And reared to God a votive shrine,
　　To man a place of rest.

And ages ere the keep of Ross
　　Frowned o'er its land-locked bay,
Or hunter's horn was heard across
　　The lake at break of day,

The convent bells rang sweet and clear
　　The early morning chime,
While echo from her airy sphere
　　Gave back each note sublime.

The Lament of Dunquin. (19).

[On the 5th of May, 1870, a dreadful catastrophe occurred from the explosion of a cask of paraffin caught by the Dunquin fishermen floating on the waves.]

Let the wild winds wail around Dunmore Head,
    And murmuring ocean boom hoarsely below,
For the heirs of the sea lie stark and dead,
    And the hearts of the living are steeped in woe.

It was not the tempest, or angry surge,
    Which stilled the strong hearts of the toiling
       brave;
No mother looked forth from the tall cliff's verge
Calling in vain for some hand to save.

Like a snake coiled up in a flowery wreath,
    Or a bandit arrayed in gentle guise,
The subtle destroyer, the angel of death
    Entered the cot as the fisherman's prize.

Smerwick, and Ventry, and Ferriter Bay
    Were crimsoned with blood in the wars of yore;
But, peace all around, a far ghastlier day
    Illumines the slaughter by Dunquin shore.

Russia's Circular.

Now face to face, upon the world's wide stage
   The two opposing Powers, brute force and right,
In view of troubled nations, fiercely wage
   The old, hereditary, fated fight
   First fought by Satan with the Lord of light,
As weird Apocalypse and Milton say;
   For force and fraud with kingly power unite
To combat public law, and wrench away
The guard of freedom dear against despotic sway.

Sound sweet-voiced Freedom! sound through all
     thy coasts,
   From Nova Zembla's weary, wintry night,
To southern climes, where England boasts
   Her latest scions. Summon to the fight,

Where'er his dwelling be, the stainless knight
Not yet extinct; and call from pole to pole
    Thy sons who better love to die outright,
Than, having reason, will, heart, mind and soul,
To bow those sovereign gifts to *one* vain man's
    control.

Rhymes on the Land.

The following " Rhymes on the Land" were written during the progress of the Land Bill through Parliament.

TO JOHN BRIGHT, ESQ., M.P.

" I have often travelled on a road and seen a hill a mile off that looked very steep but coming near the slope appeared much more gradual.   The Irish land question is not at all that sort of question."—*Mr. Bright's speech at Birmingham.*

Tho' bold and steep the mountain face
   O'erhung by many a rock,
The Saxon is a dauntless race
   And loves the alpen-stock.

Two snowy peaks rise high above
   The elemental war;
But *one** is reached, then onward move
   Crying—" *Excelsior!* "

---

* Alluding to the settlement of the Church question.

Great Tribune! ever in the van
    Of the onward march of mind,
Delay not thou the steep to scan,
    Nor cast a look behind.

Still freedom as of old delights
    To dwell apart from crowds,
Who wins her still must scale the heights,
    And bravely pierce the clouds.

Rhymes on the Land.

January 28th, 1870.

———

" The tenth Avatar comes !"—CAMPBELL.

———

Awake ! the long and weary night
   Of bondage rolls away,
And Freedom's glorious orb of light
   Is ushering in the day.

Arise ! no anger in the heart,
   But firm resolve to win
A home from which they ne'er shall part,
   For Irish kith and kin.

No more the children of the soil
   Shall meet an early grave,
Bowed down by unrequited toil,
   Or driven beyond the wave.

Justice and law shall on their way,
    Go hand in hand together,
To Cæsar we will tribute pay,
    But hold Free land* for ever.

The sickly train of town-bred ills
    Gives place to rural joys,
The echoing horn rings through the hills,
    And merry shout of boys ;
The shout of boys, the maiden's song,
    And all the world at play,
Oh ! I will join the happy throng
    And troll my roundelay !

* Commercially free, the sense in which **Mr. Bright** used
the words.

Rhymes on the Land.

February 8th, 1870.

———

The following lines were suggested by a scene at Aunascaul Petty Sessions, where the priest and people were arrayed against the proprietor of Inch island in Castlemaine bay, who claimed patent rights to the coral sand and sea-weed, to the exclusion of the public.

———

Oh! mock not thus those grand decrees
　　Which ruled creation's birth :
' The gathered waters he called seas,
　　" The dry land he called earth !"

And ne'er did sea or earth ignore
　　The sovereign, prime decree ;
The sea has washed the shingly shore,
　　The shore turned back the sea.

Still each pursues its course alone,
   True to a general plan ;
The sea yields tributes of its own
   To earth, which teems for man.

For ever within coral caves
   The living myriads toil,
And meadows grow beneath the waves
   To fertilize the soil.

Shall then monopoly control
   The boon so freely given,
Or set aside by parchment scroll
   The title-deeds of Heaven ?

Oh! let not feudal rights impair
   Or in abeyance keep
The right divine of all to share
   The blessings of the deep!

Rhymes on the Land.

February 15, 1870.

—————

WHEN shall the solid land be free,—
  Free as the viewless wind,
Free as the rolling boundless sea,
  Or thoughts that shake mankind?

Strike from the mind the leaden chains
  Of ignorance and sloth,
Wash from the heart the crimson stains
  Of envy, hate, and wrath.

Let sordid aims and party strife
  No public men defile ;
Cast from the sphere of private life
  All forms of force and guile.

Let sensual pleasures cease to sway
  The instinct and the will,
Let love alone with tempered ray
  Rain down her influence still ;

Freedom shall compass then the land,
  And search it through and through ;
Nor shall again submissive stand
  The many to the few.

Rhymes on the Land.

April 1st, 1870.

———

Where any newspaper printed in Ireland contains any treasonable or seditious engraving, matter, or expressions . . . . all printing-presses, engines, machinery, types, implements, utensils, paper, and other plant and materials used for the purpose of printing or publishing such newspaper, shall be forfeited to her Majesty, and may be seized under the Lord Lieutenant's Warrant."—*The Peace Preservation (Ireland) Act*, 1870. Secs. 27 & 28.

———

O England ! Freedom's Fatherland
    In thought, in word, in deed,
Why strike with parricidal hand
    Thy stay in every need?

What made thee great, what raised thee high
    Before the nations' eyes?
Where poets, warriors, sages, vie,
    What gives to thee the prize?

'Twas treason and sedition sped
   Fresh from the printers' mart,—
'Twas they raised up thy sov'reign head,
   And made thee what thou art.

Why at the mimic tones grow pale
   Of this thy wayward child?
Not thus did Milton's spirit quail,
   When faction revelled wild.

Oh! tell it not across the wave,
   Where thoughts and words combine
To strike the fetters from the slave,
   And make free men divine.

Rejoice ye despots of the World!
   Bind fast the toiling herd ;
Lo! slavery's banner is unfurled—
   'Tis England gives the word!

But mourn, my country, thus to thee
   The double boon assigned ;
What boots it that the land is free
   If chains are on the mind.

Rhymes on the Land.

April 8th, 1870.

The Member for East Surrey contrasted the land systems under the Irish Chieftains, the Norman Barons, and the law of contract.—(*Mr. Buxton's Speech in Committee on Clause* 3.)

WHEN Chiefs of old unsheathed the sword,
    Fast flew the signal-light,
The clansman hurried to his lord,
    And backed him in the fight.

The Land and Chief for whom he fought,
    Like coloured rays combined,—
Each with the other inly wrought,
    Were imaged on his mind.

Next comes the Norman Baron bold,
    With villein, squire and knight,
Who strike alone for what they hold,
    Whose tenure is to fight.

Then lords and vassals, rich and poor,
    Were knit by mutual ties;
None turned the wanderer from the door,
    No traitor sought disguise.

The age of barter follows next,
    When gold is all-in-all;
And naught for naught is made the text
    In cottage and in hall.

From rent alone all blessings flow,
    It measures all desert;
The open hand is nerveless now,
    The kindly heart inert.

Oh! cease that strain! see brightly burning
    The star of hope above;
The golden age is now returning,
    And universal love!

Rhymes on the Land.

ADDRESS TO THE IRISH MEMBERS BEFORE THE BATTLE.

THE trumpet-call sounds loud and clear
　　That summons to the fight;
Then, to the onset! Brothers dear,
　　And God defend the right!

Nor helm nor hauberk serves the turn
　　To champion freedom now;
"The thoughts that breathe and words that
　　　burn"
　　Must crown her glorious brow.

Oh! for the tongue of him who swayed
　　The Irish senate's ear;

Who won a wreath, too soon to fade*

    Upon his country's bier;

Or give us back for one short hour—

    A greater still than he,†

The man who broke the bands of power

    And made our altars free.

Alas! the grave yields not its own—

    Those uncrowned kings of men—

Union can weld our force alone

    And make us strong again.

Time flies, but trust not you to-morrow;

    The tide is at its flood;

This lesson take from bye-gone sorrow,

    Let faction be withstood.

* Grattan—the legislative independence of 1782 was followed
by its extinction in 1800.

† O'Connell.

So shall your names be read in story,
    The single-hearted band
Who wooed the beacon-light of glory
    And saved their native land!

Christmas, 1869.

INVITATION FROM THE KILLARNEY LADIES TO THE
CHILDREN IN THE KILLARNEY WORK HOUSE.

O WAIFS and strays! O waifs and strays
 Of this life's stormy sea!
From the highways and the byeways,
 Flock round our Christmas tree!

Come·hither boy! and quickly prove
 Our shelter from the cold;
Thou art the child of buried love,
 Cast out upon the wold.

Come hither, too, thou little maiden!
 Seek refuge in our cage,
Sent from thine own nest sorrow-laden,
 By a drunken fathers's rage.

With noiseless footstep famine steals
   Athwart the busiest mart,
But leaves behind what aye appeals
   Not vainly to the heart.

When death strikes down the stalwart arm,
   And artist's lordly head,
The orphans feel with wild alarm
   Their only stay has fled.

The poor man's cot is levelled down
   To suit the rich man's eye,
And all the tiny brood has flown
   To bide the wintry sky.

O waifs and strays! the tribute given
   From a vast sea of woe!
To us you are bequests from heaven,
   Its image here below!

O little children! here repair,
　Most worthy of our love!
For childhood's joys, like holiest prayer,
　Ascend to heaven above.

INSTRUCTIONS SUPPOSED TO BE GIVEN BY THE KILLARNEY
POOR LAW GUARDIANS FOR THE PREPARATION OF A
CHRISTMAS TREE FOR THE YOUNG INMATES. 1870.

———

' SUPPER, suffer little children; let them, let them
    come to me,'
Should be graven on each bosom, and festoon each
    Christmas Tree;
'Tis a flash of light from Heaven, 'tis a spark that
    runs through all,
From the gaily lighted salon, to the dimly lighted
    hall.

Fathers! mothers! be not anxious for too early
    ripen'd fruit,
And to teach the young idea prematurely how to
    shoot;
Knowledge is not always useful, innocence is ever
    good,

Loss of it brought banishment, and long after-
wards the flood.

Let not Wisdom, then, the branches of our merry
Christmas Tree
Load with saws and moral maxims, proud Philo-
sophy! from thee;
Fun and frolic are our masters; Fairy Queen is
mistress here,
They alone can season duly days that come but
once a year.

Here show forth in mimic marvels moving scenes
from real life,
Weddings, births, and merry meetings, frets and
jars of man and wife;
Else old Square-toes and Blue-stockings, with
mnemonics and the schools
Will but make our darling dunces mere recep-
tacles for rules.

Bring us Jack the Giant-Killer, with his comrade
    Thomas Thumb,
And a file of martial soldiers, always marching to
    the drum;
Merry Andrews, Punch and Judy, birds and
    beasts from Noah's ark,
And the other fit materials for the bird they call
    a lark.

Waxen babes, cocks, dogs, and horses, with a
    nigger here and there,
And a pretty little lady in a handsome chaise and
    pair;
Till delight on fair young faces (peals of laughter
    ringing round);
Slowly wakes to merry music, chords that long
    had ceased to sound.

Aqua Vitæ,—Uisge Beatha,—Whiskey.*

WHILST Adam dwelt in Eden yet
    And fixed by name each living thing,
He saw a bubbling diamond jet
    Beside the tree of knowledge spring.

" Water of life," our grand sire said
    " I name this brightly bubbling fount,
" Named from the tree whose branches shed
    " Perennial life o'er yonder mount."

Alas! the idly wasted breath!
    For tho' the sparkling waters flow
We find in life the cause of death,
    In good the source of many a woe.

* Perhaps few are aware that the word whiskey is a corruption of the Irish word *uisge* signifying water. It is strange that in languages which have so little affinity as the Irish and English on the one hand, with the French and Latin on the other, the name for this spirit should have the same metaphorical meaning. In Irish it is *uisge* (water), and *beatha* (life), and in the other languages named, respectively, *water of life*, *eau de vie*, and *aqua vitæ*.

An Incident of the War.

———

Oh! whither is gone from the gay Belvedere
The flaxen-haired lad with the light blue eye?
He sprang to his steed, and he couched his spear,
As he waved to his love a fond good-bye.

Oh! whither is gone from the gay Belvedere
The tender-eyed lass with the dark-flowing hair?
She gave not a sign, and she dropt not a tear
As she sped through the folds of the icy air.

On a field of snow, all spotted with red,
Where the cold moon-beams are shining, .
The youthful hussar has pillowed his head,
On her frozen breast reclining.

Mighty, unquenchable power of love!

Clear fountain and essence divine!

Her love for her lover she died to prove,

And he for their home by the storied Rhine.

Woman's Rights.

———

I SAW Aurora rise from rest
　　Where sky and ocean meet;
A pale star glittered on her breast,
　　And silver veiled her feet.

A call of joy through nature ran
　　At this enchanting sight,
And sorrow fled the heart of man
　　Before this child of light.

I saw Apollo mount the sky,
　　With bended bow in hand;
And saw his teeming arrows fly
　　Prolific through the land.

It was the merry month of May,
    And earth brought forth sweet flowers,
And man beneath the genial ray,
    Put forth diviner powers.

Dian I saw serenely move
    Across the starry maze,
And tower and town and hill and grove
    Slept in her silver haze.

And such, methought, the sov'reign plan
    Designed for woman's life,—
To cheer, to soothe, to strengthen man
    Amid the rough world's strife.

Again I saw break drear and cold
    The morning in the east;
And nature sickened to behold
    The toiling man and beast.

I saw at noon the driving rain
　　Make void the poor man's toil;
At night beheld the foaming main
　　Gather the fated spoil.

Such are the types of her who fain
　　Would mingle in the strife!
Not hers to calm a troubled brain,
　　Or smooth the path of life.

Alma Mater.

(On revisiting Trinity College, Dublin, on the 19th of February, 1871, after an absence of many years).

ALMA MATER! once again I view,
    When life has reached its autumn time,
Thy matron-grace which erst-while threw
    Its chastening spells around my prime;
Again I feel thy key unlock
    The sealed up fountains of the heart,
Again thou strik'st the arid rock,
    And forth the healing waters start.

Wise mother of enduring thought!
    Now thou dost search thy truant son,
Ask what ennobling work he wrought,
    How closed life's battle here begun;

How used thy teachings from the lore
   Gleaned from the wise and great of old;
The friends that reached his bosom's core
   Retain they still their firm-set hold?

Alma mater!—no, I will not scan
   Thy special creed; I only find
Thine is a nobly thought-out plan
   To mould and nurse the generous mind.
My hope is now that thou may'st stand,
   —Thy halls and temples—long to be
A pillar of this Irish land,
   A beacon-light of liberty.

NOTES.

---

(1). INNISFALLEN. Page 3.

INNISFALLEN is, according to Joyce, derived from Innis, an island, and Faithlen (pronounced Fahlen) a man's name. According to the same authority the small island off Howth, now known as Ireland's Eye, was antiently called Innisfallen. The island to which the poem refers is the most beautiful and most celebrated of the islands in that portion of Lough-lein, now known as the Lower Lake of Killarney. It is composed of lime-stone rock which in this district is often metamorphosed into beautiful marble. In the month of May it presents a sheet of hawthorn blossom, and in October of red berries. A monastery for Augustinian friars, of which extensive ruins still remain, was here founded about the year 550 by St. Finan, surnamed the leper. It was by its abbots that were compiled the celebrated Annals of Innisfallen, one of the oldest and most authentic of the records of Ireland now extant. These annals according to O'Curry (Lectures, p. 75) were commenced about the year 1015 and were continued down to the year 1215. It is to be regretted that no complete translation of them has as yet issued from the press. In the monastery there existed a school for youth where many of the chief men of the country received their education; the most celebrated was Brian Boroihme, the renowned conquerer of the Danes at the Battle of Clontarf. In later days the island became a place of resort for pleasure-seekers, and many a gay festival was held amid the ruins during the summer season. A pretty chapel overhanging a cliff and facing Rosse Castle became a favourite banqueting hall, and after each stag-hunt, a pastime once native to the Lakes, the walls rang with convivial merriment.

Sed tempora mutantur nos et mutamur in illis ; all but the unchangeable beauty of the island has altered with opinions and manners.

---

(2). THE SLEEP OF CUDDY. Page 8.

A LEGEND OF INNISFALLEN.

IT is related that one of the Augustinian Fathers named Cuddy, an inmate of the Monastery of Innisfallen, on a day very many centuries ago, repaired across the lake in a boat to the mainland, having the intention of shortly returning to his convent. Whilst engaged in prayer at a holy well situated on a wooded eminence overlooking Loch-lein, Cuddy was overtaken by a deep sleep, in which state he continued uninterruptedly for a period of about two hundred years. When he awoke, not being aware that he had slept for more than a few hours, he returned again by boat to Innisfallen, where he expected to join his brethren at matins, to which the summons happened just then to be sounding from the convent belfry. His astonishment, as may be imagined, was great at the changes which had occurred during his, as he supposed, short absence. The faces that met his eye were all strange; the friars spoke a language unintelligible to him; old trees had vanished, and young ones had grown into aged oaks. No one recognised him, and he was all but treated as an imposter, when it occurred to one of the more thoughtful of the community to consult the archives of the house. This led to the discovery that the new arrival was no other than the long lost Cuddy, who, according to a tradition then still current, had disappeared a couple of centuries before, and whose fate had hitherto baffled all enquiry. When Cuddy was made aware of the facts, and of the length of years to which he had attained without bodily sustenance, his whole frame collapsed, and nothing remained on the spot where he had been standing but a small heap of fine dust. The transformation was accompanied by strains of the sweetest melody floating in the air. The hard stone where

Cuddy's protracted slumber took place is still marked by the supposed impress of his knees, as any one may see who visits the spot. The same stone, from which there is no outlet, and which has no inlet, is hollow and basin-shaped. It contains, it is said, pure spring water, which, according to the legend, never fails, not even in the hottest weather or the longest summer. It is called *Cloch na Cuddy* (Cuddy's Stone), and the faith of the dwellers in the adjoining district is attested by the innumerable offerings still hung by votaries on the surrounding trees.

(3.) LEGEND OF O'DONOGHUE. Page 12.

SEVERAL versions of the O'Donoghue legend are current, which, though they vary in details, agree in representing the O'Donoghue as a powerful chieftain endowed with magical powers, who plunged from the summit of his castle into the lake beneath. A fair lady is also brought into connection with the tale in one form or another. Another pervading feature is, that the departed returns periodically to visit the scenes of his mortal pilgrimage. Moore, in his Irish melody, "O'Donoghue's Mistress," has given his version, which he probably learned during his visit to Killarney in 1824. In Florence MacCarthy's poems occurs another version, translated from the German, under the title, "The Elf-King O'Donoghue." The legend, as recounted by one versed in lake-lore, is to the effect that O'Donoghue was a great prince, endowed with wonderful magical powers, among which was that of transforming himself into the semblance of any other animal. His lovely wife, whom he tenderly loved, desired anxiously to see some manifestation of his power; and, notwithstanding his warning, that an outcry or exhibition of terror on her part would produce an eternal separation, she persevered, and at last prevailed. The legend says, that O'Donoghue, having caused a huge vessel full of water to be conveyed to the top of his castle, in the presence of his wife jumped in and transformed himself into a salmon, and swam several times around

the tub. This change the wife bore without quail-
ing, but requested a second exhibition; and her
husband then took the shape of an antlered stag,
and began to pace round the battlements, and look
down over the ledge; thereupon the wife, in her
terror, uttered a piercing cry, and the stag jumped
into the lake below, and the chief never again
appeared, except in his phantom form at stated
periods.

(4.) THE RIVER FLESK. Page 16.

THE River Flesk, flowing from an eastern direc-
tion, is one great source of supply to Loch-lein,
the other being the river flowing from the Upper Lake,
and which discharges its waters through the "Old
Weir Bridge." The scenery at this point, it is
said, particularly attracted the notice of Sir Walter
Scott, when he visited the lakes in 1825, and the
spot is always pointed out to tourists as that which
most excited the admiration of the great master.

(5.) GLEN-FLESK CASTLE. Page 18.

The residence of D. C. Coltsmann, Esq.

(6.) Page 20·

See Note 4.

(7.) THE OLD WEIR BRIDGE. Pag 21.

THE southern tributary to Loughlin flows underneath this bridge. Though mentioned in guide-books as the Long-range River, its proper name, now seldom or never used, is *Barrnasna,* so called from the old name of the Upper Lake, which discharges its over-flow through this channel.

(8.) THE EAGLE'S NEST. Page 25.

THE Eagle's Nest is too well known to require description of any kind, save that it is remarkable for the echo it gives forth as for its having been the place where the eagle had his eyrie until very recently.

" The cliff called the Eagle's nest forms a termination to a short range of mountains. . . . . It is scarcely in the power of language to convey an adequate idea of the extraordinary effect of the echoes under this cliff." . . .—*Weld's Killarney,* p. 134.

(9.) PARC AN AIFERINN—A MANGERTON HYMN.

Page 29.

ABOUT half-way up the ascent of Mangerton, a few hundred yards to the right of the road leading to the Punch-bowl, there is an enclosed field called by the mountaineers, " *Parc an Aiferinn,*" which being translated signifies the " *field of the mass.*" The peasantry answer enquiries as to the origin of the name by the statement that in the time of Cromwell, the Priest used to say Mass for the people within the field in question. There is no doubt but the name marks the precise spot where, in the days of persecution, the Priest and people assembled to cele- brate the Holy Sacrifice. The situation is secluded, but commands a view of Loch-lein and the Abbey of Irrelagh. It must be left to etymologists to assign a derivation to the word *aiferionn*, the Irish word as spelt in the nominative case, which signifies mass ; it may be remarked, however, that whilst the word " mass," or some modification of it, is embodied in almost every other European language, it appears in no shape or form in the Irish.

(10.) THE PAPS. Page 33.

TRADITION has it that a celebrated Queen of the Tuatha-de-Dananu race built a palace on the-side of the Pap mountains, the remains of which still exist and are known far and near by the name of " the

City," to which pilgrims from all parts of Ireland resort on May eve. An allusion to these venerable ruins is to be found in a note by O'Donovan in his splendid edition of the Four Masters, vol. i., p. 23, where he remarks—"The monuments ascribed by the antient Irish writers to the Tuatha-de-Danann colony still remain and are principally situated in Meath, near the Boyne, as at Drogheda, Dowth, Knowth, and New-grange. There are other monuments of them at Cnoe-Aine and Cnoe-Greine, in the county of Limerick, *and on the Pap mountains, 'Da cic Danainne,'* in the S. E. of the county of Kerry."

(11.) GLEANN-NA-COPPULL—(THE HORSE'S GLEN.)

Page 34.

GLEANN-NA-COPPULL, or, the Horse's Glen, is incomparably the finest mountain gorge in the Killarney lake district. Nothing in the Gap of Dunlo, the Black Valley, or Kippagh, approaches it in sublimity and that combination of softness and grandeur which characterise the mountain valleys in the barriers around. The glen in question is crescent-shaped, one horn resting on a plateau, half way up the side of Mangerton, the other horn penetrating into the very bowels of the same mountain, and separated by an inaccessible ledge of rock from the Punch-bowl. There are three lakes in the glen, placed in succession, one beyond the other, and each succeeding one more beautiful than the one which went before. *Lough-Gearraig*, or the bitter lake, *Lough-Managh*, or the middle lake, and *Lough-Iarraigh*, or the western lake. Around these lakes the cliffs rise in shapes of endless variety to an immense height. The ground in summer is covered with every species of wild flowers; and every variety of fern finds a nook in the endless caverns which are formed by overhanging rocks. At the top of the glen a small patch of incomparable verdure is called by the mountaineers the " *Gardene*," or little garden. Until lately this place was the abode of eagles and foxes. The name Gleann-na-

Coppull (Horse's Glen) is derived from a well-known fact, that an eagle once pursued a young foal on the heights above, and caused its fall down the precipice into the gulf beneath. Nothing can surpass the effect of the rainbow as it spans this glen. The path-way at present accessible only to good pedestrians affords by far the most picturesque approach to the top of Mangerton. In the interior are to be seen the remains of a *Still*, existing long before the R.I.C., and the debris of a slate quarry which once furnished covering to the houses in Killarney town.

(12.) BENAUNMORE. Page 35.

BENAUNMORE (the *great* hillock, as distinguished from Benaunbeg—the *little* hillock) is the name of the very remarkable conical hill, which stands at the top of Lough Guitane about 4 miles from Killarney. Its name and site may be seen on the Ordnance Map of the County Kerry. It is flanked on one side by the range of mountains of which Mangerton is the chief, and on the other by the stately Crohane. It is separated from its gigantic guardians by two extremely narrow gorges—one on either side—called respectively Esk-duive and Esk-Cael. The pedestrian, on entering the former, is introduced to a scene of surpassing loveliness and grandeur, which terminate in a perfect gem of beauty, the little lake Carrig-Veh. This name signifies the Lake of the birch covered rock, being compound of Carrig (rock) and Beith (birch). It is named on the map, but not according to the nomenclature of the mountaineers, Crohane lake. One of the most remarkable features in the scenery is communicated by the columnar structure of the rocks, which line, tier upon tier, the narrow gorge. These rocks are of volcanic origin and are, some pentagonal, others hexagonal, and have all clear and well defined outlines. They are classed by geologists as felstone, and are thus described by the late well-known professor Jukes in his Manual of Geology at page 72. " Benaunmore near Killarney columnar, greenish gray, compact with facets of felspar and globular specks of quartz." An analysis of the stone by professor Haughton is given at p. 71 of the same work. It is impossible to traverse this mountain pass on a calm day in summer without being penetrated by the sense of unutterable solitude and death-like stillness which reign around.

(13.) CARAN-TUAL. Page 37.

THE derivation of Caran-tual is the subject of controversy. The most probable is that which gives it as Carn, a monumental mound, and Tuathal (pronounced Tual), a pre-historic and celebrated Irish hero and king. The not far distant town of Listowel is admittedly derived from Lis, a fort and the same " Tual."

Caran-tual, is the highest of the M'Gillicuddy Reeks, and also the highest mountain in Ireland, being 3,256 feet above the level of the sea.   It would be difficult to match the view from this summit on a clear day.   Far away to the west is seen the Atlantic, with the headlands of Bantry-bay on the south, and Valencia Island on the north of the field of vision.   In the intervening space is stretched out a vast tract of mountains succeeding one another like the waves of the sea.   Some thousand feet below lie the recesses of the Black Valley with its cluster of small lakes, and immediately heyond Glen Carr and Cara lake whose banks are dotted round with pleasant villas.

The presiding genius of Caran-tual is emphatically "The Hag," who forms the central figure in many a tale.   This person is commemorated at every turn up the ascent.   You have the Hag's glen, the Hag's bed, and her looking-glass; the Hag's lake, her tooth, and jaw-bone.   Every guide is conversant with the history of this awful personage, whose spectre is still believed to haunt the Glen, emerging after night-fall from her abode under the waters of the lake which bears her name. On these occasions she assumes an appearance answering to the description of the celebrated sea-serpent; in this guise she is said to have almost frightened to death a small party of poachers, who, on a recent occasion happened to be following their piscatory instincts.

It is greatly to be regretted that the magnificent scenery of this mountain region is not brought within the range of ordinary pedestrians by the formation of pathways easy of ascent. We should consider it an intolerable grievance to be locked out from a picture gallery provided at the public expense; and here we have a gallery of nature's own forming, inimitable by art, from which we are shut out by the want of a little judicious outlay. A few miles of road-way through the mountains in the Lake-district would invite and multiply tourists and greatly conduce to the prosperity of the locality.

(14.) CAHER CON-RÍGH. Page 38.

THIS stone fortress stands on a pointed rock, rising 2,713 feet, almost sheer, above the glen beneath, or nearly as high as Mangerton above the sea-level. It consists of a circular stone wall, fifteen feet in thickness by 20 in height, except on the sea-side where an escarpment of rock completes the rampart. The diameter of the fort is at least 100 feet. The name Caher Con-Righ signifies in English the stone fort of King Con. From its battlements are distinctly visible to the naked eye, on the north side, Loop Head where the Shannon mingles with the sea, and on the south side the Island of Valencia, the distance between the two points as a bird would fly being 50 miles. The intervening arc of a circle is occupied by various bays and inlets, among others, by the mouth of the Shannon, Tralee and Dingle bays and Valencia Harbour. Standing within this right-royal fort, one can understand why the earliest battles recorded in Irish annals should be connected with this locality. To such a one, acquainted with the prominence given both in prose and verse, to the battles of *Slieve Mis* and *Finntraigh* (Ventry) *harbour*, the reason why becomes at once apparent. An invader's fleet steering from Spain would evidently make for one of the harbours in view, whilst it is equally clear that not a cockle-shell could float in any one of them unperceived by the watcher in King Con's tower. It remains only to add that the word Ierne is supposed by some authorities to mean the Island furthest west, and etymologists countenance the supposition by deriving the word from *iar* (west) and *inis* (island). This derivation may perhaps only be the expression of a very general conviction that the Celtic migration from the earliest times tended westward. The name however probably does mean the expression of a geographical fact.

(15). DUNLOE. Page 39.

THE Castle of Dunloe—in Irish Dun-Loich—is the residence of Daniel Mahony, a descendant of an old Milesian family. The Castle overhangs the river Laune—in Irish Leamhain—it was originally built in the year 1215 by Maurice, son of Thomas Fitz-gerald, according to a most interesting note of Dr. O'Donovan in his folio edition of the Four Masters, vol. iii., p. 188.

---

(16). AGHADOE. Page 40.

THREE circumstances claim the special attention of the visitor to this charming spot.—The panoramic view of the Lower Lake, its islands and surrounding mountains; the cluster of ruined buildings within the narrow compass of a rood or two of land; and the names of places and coterminous townlands, suggestive as they are of the antient history of the locality in the absence of all historical record. The ruins consist of a Keep or Castle once evidently of immense strength, called by the peasantry the "Caislean," whose antiquity is supposed to reach beyond even that of the neighbouring round tower; the only tradition remaining of this fortalice is, that it was battered from Ross Castle by Ludlow in the year 1652. The identical cannon which was instrumental in its demolition is still shown at Ross, with the date of 1590 inscribed, and passes by the name of the "Toothless Judy," from its jagged muzzle. The Round Tower and antient Church complete the group of ruins. Nothing is known of the date or history of either, the only trace consisting of an entry in the Annals of Innisfallen given in the Hibernicon Monasticon to the effect "that the King of Eogonacht-Lochlein died in 1231, and was buried in his old abbey at Aghadoe." The names of the place and the adjoining townlands are particularly suggestive. Aghadoe itself means the "field of the two yew trees," *Aghad* (field) *do* (two) and *eo* (yews). Immediately co-terminous with the south and west of the grave-yard is the townland of Farranaspig, or

the Bishop's land—*Farran* (land) and *aspig* (bishop).
And on the north and east of the same lies the town-
land now barbarously called Nunstown, but whose
real name is Killeen-cailaight, or the little church of
the nuns—from *Killeen* (little church) and *caillaght*
(nuns), which word again is derived from *caille*, a
veil or hood.

It is unnecessary, perhaps, to add that Aghadoe
is now the favorite burial place of all the Milesian
families for many miles around ; but it may not be
altogether unnecessary to remind the reader that the
authentic and most antient name of the Irish was
Scot, and that the existence of Prince-bishops
amongst them was not an unknown occurrence.

The copy of the Annals of Innisfallen in the Royal
Irish Academy contains at folio 138 the following
entry :—" Anno 1158.   The great Church of
Aghadoe was finished by Auliffe Mor-na-Ciummsio-
nach, Son of Aongus O Donoghue, having obtained
the supreme government of Eoganacht Loca Lein
for his posterity."

(17). THE ABBEY OF IRRELAGH. Page 41.

The Abbey of *Irrelagh* (now called Mucross Abbey) derives its ancient name from the Irish words *Oir* (East) and *Bheallagh* (pass). The legend respecting the foundation of this abbey is given in the Annals of the Four Masters, and more recently in Archdeacon Rowan's Lake Lore. It is to the effect that the M'Carthy More of the time, being desirous to found an abbey, was warned in a vision to erect it on *Carraig-an-cheol* (the rock of music), and that by supernatural agency he was directed to the spot on which the present Mucross Abbey stands and from which heavenly strains are said to have emanated. The rock on which the ruins still exist is known to this day among the peasantry as *Carraig-an-Cheol*. The foundation, according to the Annals of the Four Masters, took place in 1340, and is due to the Franciscans, the same order of men who have lately revived its glories and name in the neighbourhood of Killarney, where they have erected a splendid edifice and designated it by the name of "New Muckross Abbey." It would be equally impossible to describe the veneration of the people for the old abbey as a burial place, and for the new one as the abode of those whom they regard as their best friends. If you ask a Mangerton mountaineer why he objects to emigrate? his answer will probably be because he wishes to be buried down there in the Abbey.

---

(18). SISTER AGNES. Page 47.

THE congregation of the Sœurs du bon Secours was founded in 1824, the first vows in the congregation being pronounced on the 24th January in that year to Monseigneur de Quelin, Archbishop of Paris, who took the title of founder and head superior of the congregation. The Convent in Dublin was established on the 6th May, 1861.

(19). LAMENT OF DUNQUIN. Page 69.

" On Thursday, the 5th inst., the crew of a Dunquin boat, whilst gathering seaweed from the rocks, met with a cask of paraffin oil floating on the waves. On their return to the shore they conveyed it to the house of one of their number; and towards evening proceeded to divide the contents among the captors, who, with several of their respective families, men and women, young and old, were present on the occasion. A spark was, in utter ignorance, applied by one of the bye-standers to a portion of the oil that overflowed. An appalling explosion followed; instantaneously the cottage was shattered to pieces, and seven of the inmates reduced to cinders. The heart-rending misery and destitution resulting from the castrophe in the remote hamlet of Dunquin are indescribable." * * * *—*Abridged from the narrative of Father Egan, P. P., Ferriter.*

(21). LOCH-LEIN. Page 1.

LOUGH-*lein*. The spelling of the word *Lein* has been
adopted from the annals of the Four Masters, where
it is invariably spelled as in the text, in preference
to that used in the Ordnance Survey. The name
Lein is derived from a stream so called which
descends into the lake from Torc Mountain. The
Earl of Kenmare is proprietor under grants from the
Crown of Lough-lein. The name Kenmare—equiva-
lent to the Scotch Kenmuire—is derived from ceann
(head) and mare (sea). It signifies an estuary of the
sea. The river Kenmare forming a noble estuary of
the Atlantic, and one of the chief geographical
features in Kerry, which can be seen from all the
mountains surrounding Lough-lein by the naked eye,
gives his title to the noble proprietor of the lakes.
Mr. Joyce in his admirable book on the Irish names
of places has fallen into an error in stating "that
the town of Kenmare in Kerry received its name
from a spot on the river Roughty." That charming

little town was antiently and is still by Irish-speaking people called Nedeen signifying little nest ; but about a century since the name was changed by the Earl of Shelburne, ancestor of the present Marquis of Lansdowne, as a mark of friendship to the then Lord Kenmare. This fact is stated by Arthur Young in his *Tour through Ireland* 1776—who says, speaking of the town in question, " Lord Shelburne has a plan for improving *Nedeen, to which he has given the name of Kenmare from his friend the nobleman with that title,* which when executed must be of considerable importance," p. 287, fol. ed. 1780. It appears from lists attached to this book that Lord Shelburne was a subscriber for five copies, and also gave Arthur Young letters of introduction which are gratefully acknowledged.

CPSIA information can be obtained
at www.ICGtesting.com
Printed in the USA
BVHW081851191118
533535BV00016B/357/P